NNN - 1ᴜᴊ1
DEFER TAXES & GAIN PASSIVE INCOME WITH LONG-TERM NNN LEASES

Understanding Triple Net (NNN) Passive Income Real Estate Investments and the 1031 Tax-Deferred Exchange

By Kathy Heshelow,
Author & President of Legacy Real Estate &
Investments

NNN – 1031; Defer Taxes & Gain Passive Income with Long-Term NNN Leases. Text copyright ® 2017 by Kathy Heshelow

ISBN-13: 978-1545188965
ISBN-10: 1545188963

Published by Sublime Beauty Naturals®
11125 Park Blvd, Suite 104-103, Seminole FL 33772

GET A *FREE* AUDIO DOWNLOAD (MP3) OF AUTHOR KATHY HESHELOW EXPLAINING NNN INVESTMENTS

+ a 1031 WORKSHEET

(determine your capital gains & tax liability)

https://goo.gl/xTMWBn

Enjoy! Kathy Heshelow

WHO IS THIS BOOK FOR?

This book is for anyone who is selling investment real estate in the United States, who wants to defer the taxes of that sale, and who intends to reinvest in passive-income, little-to-no-management commercial properties, like Walgreens or Starbucks.

The book explains what the IRS 1031 Tax-Deferred Exchange is, the requirements and how to use it; and what Triple-Net NNN properties are, how to evaluate them, what pitfalls to avoid, and how the whole thing can work for you.

In this book, I share my knowledge and long experience in this fascinating niche. I have been involved with NNN investment properties and 1031 tax-deferred exchanges since the late 1990's.

When I started to work in commercial real estate, first at a top firm in Sarasota, Florida, my mentor told me, "After working with and handling all different types of commercial real estate, find one type of real estate and niche you love, immerse yourself and specialize in only that."

I followed his advice. For one year, I handled transactions in land, warehouses, commercial properties, businesses such as restaurants, office leases, apartments and more. I found my love of single-tenant NNN investment properties then. And going even further, I moved that specialization to only acting as a buyer's broker – that is, helping and representing buyers of passive-income NNN properties vs. listing and selling them. I help guide buyers and take away much of the confusion, pain and problems that could arise. Due to IRS requirements, there is stress and many pitfalls.

I have closed in excess of $170M in NNN properties (most of the investors were conducting a 1031 tax-deferred exchanges). I have learned tips, tricks and knowledge that investors can benefit from In fact, learning about the 1031 tax-deferred exchange can be enlightening to many.

Most of my books are focused, concise and to the point, and this one is no exception. I jump right in, share information that you can use, and help you understand the niche.

I hope you enjoy the book! Reach out with any questions!

Kathy Heshelow, founder & President
Legacy Real Estate & Investments
NNN Specialist
tel: 866-891-1031
Email: info@kathyheshelow.com
www.LegacyNNN.com
Facebook: www.facebook.com/legacynnn

"Anyone may arrange his affairs so that his taxes shall be as low as possible; he is not bound to choose that pattern which best pays the treasury. There is not even a patriotic duty to increase one's taxes.

Over and over again the Courts have said that there is nothing sinister in so arranging affairs as to keep taxes as low as possible. Everyone does it, rich and poor alike and all do right, for nobody owes any public duty to pay more than the law demands."

~~ ***Judge Learned Hand**, Helvering v. Gregory, 69 F.2d 809, 810 (2d Cir. 1934), aff'd, 293 U.S. 465 (1935)*

TABLE OF CONTENTS

CHAPTER 1
WHAT ARE NNN OR TRIPLE-NET LEASED PROPERTIES?

Let's get to the meat of the matter right away. Triple-Net leased properties (NNN is the typical nickname) are a very specific type of commercial investment real estate. The name refers to the lease, as you will soon learn!

1) NNN are typically single-tenant retail properties (with tenants like Walgreens, Advanced Auto, Starbucks or Burger King) though some office or warehouse NNN properties do exist.

2) Each NNN property typically has a long-term lease, such as 15 to 20 years main term with "options to renew".

3) The specific kind of lease dominates everything: in a true NNN lease, the tenant (such as Walgreens) pays not only the monthly rent, but also the insurance, taxes, maintenance, upkeep and anything to do with the property.

4) Guarantees to make payment and honor all terms of the lease can come from a corporate entity (best, if the tenant is a credit-rated – like S&P, high net worth company); from a franchisee (which can be large and credit-worthy down to small and not so much); or from a single "mom and pop" operation, like a fast-food place for instance.

5) The rate of return (cap rate) for the NNN niche of investments will be lower for the highly-rated desirable properties (like Walgreens), and higher or better for the riskier type of properties that may not have a good guarantee, or have geographic challenges or a good property with a shorter lease term, for instance.

In the passive income net-leased world, there is also what is called Double Net (NN) and even a Single Net (N) leased investments. Double Net typically means that the tenant will pay for everything except roof and structure, which would be your responsibility. Many Starbucks properties are NN. There are fewer single net deals out there, but these leases could represent any number of responsibilities for the owner/landlord (you). It would always be clear in the lease.

BEWARE: some brokers may call a property NNN - but it might not be (it might be a double-net or a single-net)! There may be some financial responsibility by you (the landlord and owner). Some in the NNN world call a property with no landlord responsibility a "True Triple Net" as opposed to just a "Triple Net". (This can be confusing!)

I find this happens less often now, but nevertheless it is good to know. Inexperienced brokers who have never dealt with the NNN world may call their listing a triple net offering, but it is not. Everything boils down to the lease, so the first thing I always check is the lease details and always ask the listing broker specifically about terms and responsibilities to see what the real story is on the property and lease responsibilities.

BENEFITS AND DISADVANTAGES

Triple Net investments **are one of the most sought after** in commercial real estate, and for good reason. No (or very little) management and involvement is needed by the investor, the leases are quite long compared to most other types of leases, and a nice, steady, passive monthly income are among the top reasons. Here are a few of the benefits:

a) No daily hassles or management to deal with at the property frees you up for your other pursuits. The tenant (such as Walgreens) is in charge of everything at the property – taxes, insurance, management, upkeep, repairs, rent, etc.

b) Many investors like the aspect of tax deductions with owning real estate, plus the kind of stability it could offer as compared to many other types of non-real estate investments (like stocks, bonds, funds or other instruments of this type.)

c) Investors WITHOUT much real estate experience like NNN investments because they will not be involved in all the details of typical ownership. This is an entirely different investment than owning and managing an apartment complex, strip mall or commercial property.

c) Those WITH real estate experience understand how much easier owning this type of property is. No bothersome calls day or night, no managing fixes, problems or issues at the property, no dealing with a turn-table of tenants, rent collections and such.

d) GEOGRAPHY. Because these are "NO MANAGEMENT" types of investments, investors have the flexibility of buying properties anywhere they wish. This can give flexibility to buy in "no tax" states, or near their grown children, or in geographic locations they desire. They aren't stuck buying something within driving distance, in other words.

e) With many NNN properties, **there is a true "pride of ownership"** aspect. The newly-built, shiny property with a top S&P rated tenant and a showcase location can fall into this category.

f) STABILITY. The relatively long-term leases (15-20 years or more with renewals) can give peace of mind and stability. That is to say, not having to worry about if a tenant will renew next year, or finding a new tenant next month, because the lease is 20 years long.

g) Corporate-guaranteed NNN properties are a little stronger during economic downturns. In the wake of 2008 when everything crashed and continued to be dour for some years, my clients with corporate NNN deals continued to collect their monthly income without a hiccup. (Not so for the mom & pop site, that went out of business and the monthly income with it.) Most clients are wise to stick with corporate guarantees. Those with deep pockets and deep experience could risk something of less quality, if they see the deal as a real estate play.

h) Banks like to lend on NNN deals, especially corporate-guaranteed ones, so terms could be better or more advantageous over some other types of real estate (less risk to the bank.)

i) There are few surprises with NNN properties, unlike dealing with active-management properties when variables and expenses can change on a daily or monthly basis.

DISADVANTAGES

But not everything is perfect and there are some disadvantages. As you will see, much will be gauged by your own point of view.

a) First, for new investors, **real estate is by nature NOT liquid.** It is not easy to quickly move in and out of most real estate investments. This statement is true for ALL types of real estate, not just NNN. And while NNN properties might sell faster than other types of real estate (depending on the tenant, location, pricing, etc.), it is still illiquid. Now let's move on to NNN specific issues.

b) While the NNN lease guarantees a rental payment month in and month out, **you are locked in to whatever the lease states** for the long haul. While some may see this as a benefit ("no surprises, no ups or downs, protection"), others will say that there is no wiggle room for more upside during the lease hold, or no negotiation over terms.

c) Many NNN leases offer a rent increase every 5 or 10 years (some are annual or even every 2 years), and most offer increases in renewal periods - but **a few are "flat" with no increases** at all during the initial lease (like Walgreens). Cost of living should go up, but not the lease income to you. This can be a tradeoff for having a solid tenant with guaranteed lease. Some view the fact of no or little upside in a lease term more as like holding a bond, a very conservative play.

d) **NNN rates of return (cap rates) are typically lower than in some other types of real estate** (but of course, you are working to manage those other types of real estate.) For instance, you might have a 6% rate of return on a strongly guaranteed NNN deal, and you may be able to get a 9% + rate of return on that apartment building you own. But remember to compare apples to apples: the out-of-pocket costs to you in those others types of leases, shorter terms, and of course the management – whether you do it (time is money) or pay someone else to.

e) **Decent NNN deal prices typically start in the two or three million dollar range: there are a few that could fall in the**

$1M +/- range, many stronger deals in the $3M-$5M range and very strong deals in the higher range. Larger deals get better mortgage terms, but you typically need about 30% down-payment for any financing (this often comes from the sale of your "relinquished" property in the case of a 1031).

f) A disadvantage could be changing geographics & demographics during your hold period. For instance, you may have bought that NNN fast food property when its location was hot and in the best area of town, but 20 years later when the lease is up, the hot area might have moved somewhere else. Of course, this is a locational risk in any type of real estate investment.

g) **While some investors buy a new 20 year leased property**, garner income and tax benefits and then sell it five years later with 15 years on the lease to a new buyer (as it is still desirable), others will hold their NNN deal for the entire lease term and onward to the renewal period. The property is typically paid off by lease end, so there is less risk if the tenant may move on or not.

Both hold strategies offer risk and reward – and much of this is out of your hands. If the markets are such that you can make money by selling in a few years (the NNN market cap rates, increase to the rent, appreciation, general real estate and economic trends are all up) then great. But if things are not moving much, selling after 4 or 5 years might not make sense or offer little profit. It may depend on the kind of mortgage you have locked in as well – some mortgages will have a pre-payment penalty if you pay off early, for instance.

Likewise, some will hold the property for the entire 20 years and then get a renewal from the same tenant and continue onwards … but others might then have an empty building because the tenant did not renew. This could be an opportunity or a problem. The opportunity could be to sell outright at a profit, or to find a new tenant (corporate or not) for continuing income; the problem could be a slow sales period or not finding a tenant, or if values have dropped, losses. You typically want to have paid off the mortgage before the end of the lease term, to reduce risk and out of pocket monies.

DIFFERENT TYPES OF NNN INVESTMENT PROPERTIES

Considering which type of NNN property you want to buy will often depend on your personal preferences. For instance, I have some clients who only want to buy so-called **dollar stores** (there are several large corporations) because they believe that whether the economy is up or down, people like a deal and will always shop in these types of stores. But I have others who tell me never to present a dollar store to them, as they don't like the locations or the way the buildings are made.

I have clients who know that no matter the economy, people need to eat and so they like to invest in **restaurants**; while others don't want to ever own a NNN restaurant (either they don't like the fact of unhealthy "fast food", or some told me they find risk in the beef markets or chicken markets, or because they are smaller square footage size than other types of NNN deals).

Other clients want the security of a strongly-rated **Walgreens** so they can sleep at night because of the strength of the tenant, and others who would never consider them because the rents are flat and the cap rates are the lowest of NNN deals.

I have clients who will ONLY buy in non-tax states (Alaska, Florida, Nevada, South Dakota, Texas, Washington and Wyoming) while others only want specific states where they reside, or where they vacation, or because they like a specific city (like Atlanta).

I have clients who only like to buy a NNN property on a **retail pad in a shopping center**, or surrounded by certain type of other retail "draws" (like Home Depot, WalMart or a grocery store), while others only want an entirely free-standing property on a corner or easy access/visibility area without worrying about the health of the shopping center.

Some love **auto parts stores**, again because they believe that most people need these type of stores (and their products) and demand is high in any economy. The same with highly-rated **banks**.

Some clients will only consider S&P rated tenants, while others will consider high-net worth franchisees who guarantee the lease. These franchises may be corporations that have 1000 stores, or

350 stores or 50 stores under their wing, for instance, and great experience. I typically only recommend this if the financials are available to evaluation, and there is monthly reporting and transparency.

Only a few of my clients ever consider mom & pop places, and they tend to be high net worth investors who don't mind the risk and want the trade-off of higher returns on their investment, because they like the particular location and value. These investors have the capability of taking on a vacant building and the obligations that go with it – they have weighed the location and opportunities in the event of a tenant failure.

Likewise, no client I have worked with in 17 years ever chose a **Zero Cash Flow** NNN property. These are high-end deals with debt that matches the income, giving a zero cash flow. It can be used for tax advantages (zero income for taxes, claiming of depreciation deductions to advantage, lower down payment for the loan.) I have seen situations where it would make sense for a company or high-net worth investor to do this, but for the most part, investors do like the cash flow!

Some like **NNN ground leases**. Ground leases are land leases, and it means that the investor owns the land only and then leases out the land to a tenant like Walgreens, Jared Jewelers or Home Depot. Many ground leases have what is called "reversionary rights", where the building reverts to the landlord/land holder at the end of the lease.

On the other hand, a "leasehold" agreement, in my opinion, is horrible (unless you are the ground holder)! You, the investor, hold the building for the lease term with monthly income, but at the end of the lease, the building reverts to the land owner. You have nothing!

However, it seems the majority of investors like to acquire what is called "**Fee Simple**", that is, ownership of the land and building, with full title.

These are just examples to show you that while NNN type of investments are very specific, there are many varieties and intricacies involved. If you are going to consider investing in a NNN deal, the first thing I suggest is to weigh your desires, your financial situation, how you feel about certain types of industries and locations. How much do you expect to get in monthly and annual income? How much upside are you expecting over time? How much equity do you expect to have from the sale of a property (or have put aside) and how much of a mortgage do you wish to have? (Some of my clients only want a 50% loan to value, while others like the philosophy of maxing as much as possible to "let other people's money work for you".) If you are considering a NN deal, how much money in reserve do you have if you need to fix a roof? These are questions that are important to consider. It's the first thing I discuss when working with a client.

The next issue is timing of your transaction, and since many NNN investors are in fact conducting an **Internal Revenue Code (IRC) 1031 Tax-Deferred Exchange**, this is a good time to move to Chapter 2 and discuss the 1031! Timing is very tight and crucial to the 1031, as you will learn, and it is easy for tax-deferral to fail without proper planning.

CHAPTER 2
THE IRC 1031 TAX-DEFERRED EXCHANGE

The author is not a tax attorney, qualified intermediary or tax expert. This chapter looks at the history and commonly-known mechanics of the 1031 tax-deferred exchange, and has been included to help the uninitiated understand what a 1031 exchange is and how it could benefit them. While the author will directly quote IRS publications, she recommends that the reader consult one of the many professionals or publications that specialize in this complex and specific subject if they wish to conduct a tax-deferred exchange.

Since many investors who acquire Triple Net Investment properties (NNN) use the 1031 as a strategic solution, reviewing the tax-deferred exchange is essential to the subject! While many real estate investors across the United States are aware of this powerful strategy, there are still many who are just discovering it.

Typically when you sell a property, you pay taxes on the capital gains. In some cases, this can be incredibly high. For instance, an investor bought a rental property in the 1970s or 1980s at a low price (let's say $25,000) and today is able to sell it for $1,100,000. (I have had clients in this very situation – the location of the property, maybe on the water or in a higher-end neighborhood.) Assuming a tax rate of 15%, the tax on the gain (profit) of $1,075,000 would be $161,250. Or, if an investor bought a property for $1,000,000 and five years later sells it at $1,250,000, the 15% tax on the $250,000 would be $37,500. Now, the tax rate goes up depending on the tax bracket and could be 25% or even 35%.

If you were planning to reinvest the funds into growing your real estate portfolio, there is a way to defer the tax. Many investors use this strategy to continue building their net worth and real estate holdings in an advantageous way. This is the 1031 tax-deferred exchange.

WHAT IS THE 1031 EXCHANGE?

The 1031 tax-deferred exchange is sometimes also known as a Like-Kind Exchange, the Starker Exchange, Delayed exchange, the IRC 1031 or simply 'a 1031'? It is the sale or disposition of property and the acquisition of 'like-kind' property following the rules and structure of Section 1031 of the Internal Revenue Code (IRC) in order to DEFER federal tax, capital gain and depreciation recapture taxes.

The term "like-kind" as applied to real estate is essentially any type of <u>investment</u> real estate with a few exceptions, such as a personal residence. This means you can sell an office building and buy a retail center or land to defer the taxes; you can sell an apartment building and buy a NNN property or industrial building to defer the taxes; you can sell a rental triplex and buy a small hotel to defer the taxes.

<u>Educated investors know that they never need pay the tax on their capital gains if they intend to reinvest sale funds into more investment property</u>, and that they can DEFER the tax due by reinvesting the proceeds into another investment property. This is not a tax free transaction - it is a deferral which can go on indefinitely and for any number of exchanges, until the day an investor or his heirs decide they will cash out and pay the tax.

The IRS specifically states in their code: **"No gain or loss shall be recognized on the exchange of property held for productive use in a trade or business or for investment, if such property is exchanged solely for property of like-kind which is to be held either for productive use in a trade or business or for investment."**

Section 1031 <u>does not apply</u> to exchanges of inventory, stocks, bonds, notes, other securities or evidence of indebtedness, or most other assets. However, it does or could apply to some business and personal property such as planes, boats, or trucks. However, for purposes of this book, we are discussing real estate to real estate.

A LITTLE HISTORY!

(Thanks to Robert L. Sommers, Journal of Taxation, a publication of Warren, Gorham & Lamont, for much of the history in this section. It is included with permission and thanks.)

Section 1031 of the Internal Revenue Code ("IRC") has a rather long and complicated history dating back to 1921. The first income tax code was adopted in 1918 as part of The Revenue Act of 1918, but did not provide for any type of tax-deferred exchange. The first tax-deferred exchange was authorized as part of The Revenue Act of 1921 when the United States Congress created Section 2021 of the Internal Revenue Code. Between 1921 and 1970, 1031 exchanges were always *simultaneous swaps* between two parties, and between 1921 and 1924 they also included non-like-kind properties.

The Section number applicable to the tax-deferred exchange was changed from 2021 to Section 112(b)(1) with the passage of The

Revenue Act of 1928. The 1954 Amendment of the Tax Code changed the Section number to Section 1031 of the Internal Revenue Code, and many of our present language and procedural details   were   adopted.

We can thank the Starker family for the rise of the 'deferred exchange'. The Starker case in 1979 gave rise to the so-called *"deferred or non-simultaneous exchange"*, the very format that almost every investor uses today. This was an important case.

The taxpayer, T. J. Starker, transferred timber property which was free and clear of debt to Crown Zellerbach Corporation in exchange for an unsecured promise by Crown to transfer to him like-kind property chosen during a 5-year period. At the end of this 5-year period, Mr. Starker would receive any outstanding balance in cash. When the transaction was set up and the property transferred to Crown, a trust agreement was formed whereby the sale proceeds would be held in a separate bank account. The terms of the trust stated clearly that the funds could only be used to purchase the replacement property for the Starker family and for no other purpose. Neither the Starker family nor Crown had access to the funds, except for buying the replacement properties.

When the IRS saw this arrangement, they denied the tax deferral. The IRS argued that a 1031 exchange meant the swap of property between two parties simultaneously. Remember, trades up to this point were always simultaneous swaps. The job of the IRS is to collect taxes and enforce the regulations (as they understand them), and so they fought against the Starker arrangement.

Starker took the case to court. The Ninth Circuit Court, in a monumental decision, ruled in favor of the Starker family and against the IRS. The Ninth Circuit found that IRC Section 1031 did not contain the requirement of simultaneity and that an exchange today for like-kind property five years in the future was permissible. The Court also stated that Mr. Starker's possibility of receiving cash in the future did not cause the transaction to fail under Section 1031.

Now, instead of having to find someone to simultaneously swap property with (risky at best and quite complicated to accomplish), investors could sell a property today to a buyer and exchange the proceeds into another property from someone else in the future. This was and is a far more practical procedure.

However, it also became an administrative nightmare for the IRS. The IRS could see that if property could be sold to one person today and bought from another later, then the application of the law could become not only quite complicated but hard to manage.

So in 1984 and 1986, Congress decided to limit the Starker decision with the Deficit Reduction Act of 1984 and The Tax Reform Act of 1986. <u>Essentially, the deferred exchange was "codified" and time limitations were defined.</u> Those limitations stipulate that an investor has 45 days from the day of selling his relinquished property to identify property or properties he will buy; he has a total of 180 days to close on one or more of those identified properties. Congress also amended Section 1031(a)(2) of the Internal Revenue Code to disallow exchanges of partnership interests.

The Tax Reform Act of 1986 marks the start of what has become an explosion in the amount of 1031 exchange transactions seen today. The Tax Reform Act of 1986 eliminated preferential capital gain treatment so that all capital gains were taxed as ordinary income; enacted passive loss and at risk rules; eliminated accelerated depreciation methods and replaced this with straight line depreciation consisting of 39 years for commercial property and 27.5 years for residential property. These changes significantly changed the benefits of owning real estate and made the 1031 exchange one of the few tax benefits left for real estate investors.

Eleven years after the Starker decision permitted deferred like-kind exchanges and six years after Congress' actions in response to the Starker decision, the Internal Revenue Service itself finally published proposed regulations intended to answer myriad unresolved issues. Many tax experts say that the regulations are relatively clear, well stated and for the most part consistent with the body of case law interpreting Section 1031.

WHAT ARE THE BASIC RULES YOU NEED TO KNOW?

The IRS rules must be followed when conducting a 1031 <u>with no exceptions</u>, and there are general mechanics that all investors should know.

If you break one of the rules, the exchange is 'disallowed' and you pay the capital gains. Here are the three most basic rules:

1) You have 45 days from the closing of your "relinquished property" (the property you are selling and deferring tax on) to identify property or properties you intend to reinvest in.

2) You have 180 days from the closing of your "relinquished property" to actually close, or else you will pay the taxes.

3) A Qualified Intermediary must hold the funds for the 1031 exchange, and transfer them at closing for your reinvestment property.

When you decide that you are going to sell an investment property, you will want to see if there will be sufficient capital gain involved with that 'relinquished property' to make a 1031 worth the effort. This will help determine if it makes sense to do a 1031 in the first place –that is, if you were planning to reinvest in more investment property or a 'replacement property'. Your accountant, financial planner or attorney can help you determine your capital gains if you cannot.

DETAIL: THE QUALIFIED INTERMEDIARY (YOU CANNOT HOLD OR TOUCH YOUR FUNDS IN THE 1031)

The Qualified Intermediary (often referred to as the QI) or exchange accommodator is the professional third party who must hold the proceeds of your sale in escrow. You the investor/seller/exchanger do not 'touch' the funds – or else you pay the tax.

The QI will handle the specific paperwork necessary for the transfer before you sell your property, assist you with "identification of property" you will purchase or intend to purchase for the exchange, hold the funds in trust, and then transfer the funds for acquisition of your chosen properties, along with other important details. The QI will coordinate with you, the title company or attorney handling the sale and your broker.

Find your QI well BEFORE you sell your property, ideally before you go into contract on the property you will sell. There are banks, title companies and attorneys who act as Qualified Intermediaries and your broker can usually refer several. There were plentiful QI companies up to 2008, but the 1031 market (reinvestment markets) fell off the face of the earth and there was no velocity, so many went away. (I tend to like entities that are regulated in the holding of funds.) In fact, the national association, Federation of Exchange Accommodators, lists all members on their website (www.1031.org).

The contract for your relinquished property (the property you are selling) should contain some specific exchange language. An example of this language is: *Buyer is aware that the sale of the subject property is part of an IRC 1031 tax-deferred exchange. Buyer agrees to an assignment of the Sellers interest in this purchase contract to a Qualified Intermediary to effect the exchange. No additional costs or liabilities will be incurred on the part of the Buyer.*

Investors should know that there are **no exceptions to the rules for dates and deadlines**, <u>even if specific dates fall on a Sunday or holiday</u>. The investor **must identify the properties with the QI that they may or will buy by calendar day 45** from the day the relinquished property sold. The **investor must close on one or all of the identified properties no later than calendar day 180** from the day the relinquished property sold. The time limits imposed by the IRS are absolutes. If you are one day or one hour late, your trade is disqualified and you will pay the tax.

THERE ARE THREE WAYS TO "IDENTIFY" PROPERTIES

There are several choices **for identification of the properties to acquire**. The QI will supply the instructions, and the registered representative or broker can assist:

1) **The Three Property Rule**. Identify up to three properties of any value. Acquire 1, 2 or all 3 of the properties. *Most choose this option.* It is wise to use all three slots even if you intend to

acquire only one property – you will have backup options in case something goes awry with choice 1.

2) **The 200 Percent Rule**.   Identify four or more properties, whose value cannot exceed twice (200%) of the relinquished property value.   Exceeding the 200% limit will disallow your transaction. *A few choose this option.*

3) **The 95% Rule**.   Identify any number of properties with an aggregate fair market value exceeding 200% of the relinquished properties and acquire virtually all (at least 95% of them, based on the total fair market value). We have seen this in the acquisition of lots by developers, as an example. *Very few choose this option.*

Identifying replacement property is relatively straightforward, and the Qualified Intermediary will assist (they usually supply specific forms to use). **The designation must be made in a written document signed and dated by the exchanger.**

It must be delivered or transmitted to the QI no later than midnight of day 45 - often a fax is preferred, because it includes a date and time in the fax receipt document though email has become accepted. The IRS regulations state that street addresses or property descriptions used must be unambiguous.   Usually identification of a NNN property includes the property name, property address, sales amount (equity and debt).

NEXT RULE TO REMEMBER: TAKING TITLE

In a 1031 exchange, **you must take title to the new property in exactly the same way you held title** in the relinquished property, whether it is you personally or an entity such as a trust, corporation, partnership, or LLC. Otherwise, the trade fails and you pay the taxes.

IMPORTANT RULE: YOU MUST "MEET OR BEAT" YOUR DEBT AND EQUITY FOR A FULL DEFERRAL

You **must replace both equity and debt at the same amount or greater** when exchanging into the replacement property, if you wish to defer the capitals gains in full.

Now, you do not have to place all of your proceeds into a new property, but whatever you take out will be taxed. You need to replace the same amount of financing or greater, but if you do not wish to do so, you are permitted – you simply will have a tax obligation on the difference. If you add new cash out of your pocket, you can reduce the financing; in other words, new cash can replace mortgage boot. (Mortgage boot cannot ever replace cash).

These are the basic concepts to know. Please do consult one of the professionals who specialize in the 1031 exchange for full details, especially relating to your specific situation. The full IRS code can be found on the IRS website.

SOME FAQs ABOUT THE 1031

Question: Do I have to invest the exact amount of money that I received from the relinquished property?

To defer capital gains, you must invest the exact amount or more (that is, "meet or beat" your equity and debt).

Question: So can I keep some of the cash from the sale of the relinquished property but exchange the rest?

Yes, but you will pay capital gains tax on the amount of cash that you take. Make sure to coordinate with the QI or your accountant so that it is done properly.

Question: I recently sold an investment property and have the funds in my money market account. Can I still do a 1031 exchange?

No, it is too late. The exchange must be set up so that your proceeds are held by the third party in assignment, and those funds are used to purchase your new property. You cannot 'touch' the funds, so to speak.

Question: Can I use 1031 proceeds to pay down a mortgage and defer tax, or perhaps make improvements to investment real estate I own with the proceeds and defer tax?

No. Paying down a mortgage is not considered 'like kind' nor is making improvements to a property you already own with one exception concerning construction leasehold exchanges.

Question: What is "boot"?

"Boot" is anything of value exchanged which is not "like-kind" to the relinquished property. This is usually cash or mortgage debt used to equalize the transaction.

Question: Can I sell one large property and buy several smaller ones?

Absolutely! An investor may sell many properties and buy one, or sell one and buy many – it is the equity and debt that must be replaced, not the number of properties, and fulfilling the time requirements. You must follow the identification rules.

Question: What if the property was held in a Trust or owned by a corporation, or what if a Partnership or LLC wants to do a 1031 with investment property they own?

No problem but remember that the entity on title of the relinquished property is the entity in which you must take title on your new investment.

Question: Can my own attorney or CPA serve as my Qualified Intermediary?

Typically not. A Qualified Intermediary must remain completely independent and cannot have been your agent in the past 2 years. A few states may have an exception.

Question: Is there a limit to the number of exchanges I can do in a year? I have several properties that I want to sell.

No, there is no limit specified. Just make sure that the properties are indeed investment properties that were 'acquired and held for productive use in a trade or business'.

Question: Is the 1031 exchange only for capital gains?

No. The 1031 applies to capital gains taxes (15%), depreciation recapture (25%), and state income taxes (generally 8% to 9% where applicable). Long-term capital gains taxes apply to property held over 1 year – gains from property held less than a year are taxed as ordinary income.

Question: Can any of the expenses for investing be deducted from the 1031 proceeds without incurring any tax consequence?

Although the IRS has not published a complete list of qualifying expenses, there are some rulings and case history. Transaction costs may be deducted if they are paid in connection with an exchange (Letter Ruling 8328011). Brokerage commission can be deducted. Direct costs of selling real estate include title insurance, legal fees, notary fees, closing or escrow fees, recording fees.

Any cost to acquire a loan cannot be deducted (mortgage points, assumption fees, credit reports, mortgage insurance, etc.). Other non-exchange expenses include such things as property taxes, insurance, association fees, and utility charges. Your QI and/or your accountant will help you with these line items.

Question: How will I handle my 1031 at tax time? How will I account for it?

You will use TAX FORM 8824 entitled Like-Kind Exchanges, among other things. Your accountant will walk you through this as they handle your returns, or the QI can assist, and there are detailed instructions with Form 8824. Make sure to save all information and closing statements, as your accountant will need these.

Question: What if I don't identify property by the deadline, or can't purchase what I identified, or decide not to do the 1031 after I have started the process? What happens to my funds held with the QI?

The right to receive your funds is actually limited. If you didn't identify anything by day 45, your funds can then be released after day 45. If you have identified property but were unable to acquire or buy, you will go through a process with your QI before funds can be released. Otherwise, the funds are not available until after the 180 day expiration.

To end this chapter, know that there are a few lesser known kinds of 1031 exchanges which are not used much, such as reverse exchanges (whereby the replacement property is purchased first, and then the relinquished property is sold), construction (improvement, leasehold or build-to-suit) exchanges, simultaneous exchanges, etc. A full book could easily be written about the 1031 exchange (many have been!), and I recommend those who are interested to know more about these other types of less common exchanges should speak with their attorney, a Qualified Intermediary, and/or review the many good books on the subject if you are going to delve deeper into the subject yourself.

CHAPTER 3
PASSIVE INCOME FROM NNN INVESTMENTS

Passive income is something that many investors of all ages like, and it is often a choice take by those who approach retirement.

The U.S. Internal Revenue Service categorizes income into three broad types, active income, **passive income**, and portfolio income. It defines passive income as only coming from two sources: rental activity (real estate income) or "trade or business activities in which you do not materially participate."

Obviously, active income means you are doing something in order to receive that income – typically being employed, making a hands-on active effort to earn revenues and profits. Passive income means you are earning regular income with little to no effort.

Today many investors like to diversify into some passive income properties. And baby-boomers are among the biggest group doing this. NNN are the ultimate PASSIVE INCOME GENERATORS with great tax benefits.

Owning real estate is great, but many don't want to actively manage property (or don't have the time). Or they have done so and are finished with it and want something that is "hands-off". In fact, many investors have put more than their share of time in on the "3 T's" – trash, toilets and tenants!

Relatively new commercial real estate investors are looking for passive income (and maybe tax deferral – perhaps they inherited some real estate and want to sell it for income property.) New investors may not have deep real estate experience. Inexperienced real estate investors can step into a NNN investment with relative ease (no, it's not all simple, but it is relatively simply.)

Selling off those management properties may mean big tax burdens, so a 1031 exchange and a way to get passive income makes sense to many in this situation.

Gaining cash flow from an asset with tax benefits can be very helpful, adding to income or retirement income. Younger investors might like the freedom, especially if they are running online businesses or working at companies that allow them travel and movement. Older investors might want to travel or be free and enjoy retirement, away from daily hassles – but still get the tax benefits and income.

Some like to diversify their "paper investments" of stocks and bonds. Some financial planners suggest that real estate should be part of an investor's portfolio if there are appropriate funds and if this fits into the strategy.

Some people at retirement age may have seen their retirement fund diminished after the 2008 crash. The fact is that the markets (and real estate markets too) will always go up and down. The difference is that real estate moves slower and has a few factors in play that are different – they are "brick & mortar" properties with intrinsic value versus a paper investment that can go away with nothing left. Add a NNN guaranteed lease from an S&P rated company guarantor, and that value can be enhanced.

In addition, investors who decide to go the route of real estate get tangible benefits from their investment, such as sheltering of the income they collect each month, depreciation, and the tax deferral at sale if they chose a 1031 exchange.

LEVERAGE!

Leverage is another positive factor in real estate (all types, including NNN) vs most other types of investment.

An investor with $100,000 can purchase $100,000 of stocks, bonds or mutual funds. An investor with $100,000 can purchase $300,000 or more of commercial real estate. Leverage is an advantage in real estate.

Leverage is defined as the use of borrowed money to increase your profits in an investment. Building wealth in real estate is usually accomplished or aided by financing. Because more money is invested overall, leverage significantly increases the percentage of profit you can make. Leverage or financing allows you to purchase a much larger investment than you would normally have been able to.

Some S&P rated NNN properties could be financed with *non-recourse debt*, the advantageous kind of debt for investors. Non-recourse financing is a type of loan in which the only remedy available to the lender in the event of the borrower's default is to foreclose on the collateral; the borrower (you) is not personally liable for repayment and you are not responsible. There are more reporting requirements (either quarterly or annually) and typically locked-in prepayment penalties in these types of loans (because of securitization), but the interest rate is very low. Expect lots of paperwork – there is some pain for the pleasure of a secure loan.

But some investors are just as happy to deal with the local bank!

CHAPTER 4
REAL ESTATE CYCLES
The Tide Turns Again

Bad times follow good times, which turn bad and then good again. Cycles in the economy and in real estate are a reality. Commercial real estate has tended to fare better over the long term, but it too can take big hits like in the carnage of 2008 and the years that followed.

General real estate markets, economy, cycle – banks, values, ups and downs.

Recession

Panic of 1857	**1857-1860**	**3**
years		
Panic of 1873	**1873-1879**	**6**
years		
Long Depression	**1873-1896**	**23**
years		
Panic of 1893	**1893-1896**	**3**
years		
Panic of 1907	**1907-1908**	**1**
year		
Post-World War I recession 1918-1921		**3**

		years
Great Depression	1929-1939	10 years
Recession of 1953	1953-1954	1 year
Recession of 1957	1957-1958	1 year
1973 Oil Crisis	1973-1975	2 years
Early 1980s recession	1980-1982	2 years
Early 1990s recession	1990-1991	1 year
Early 2000s recession	2001-2003	2 years
Economic crisis of 2008	2007-present	ongoing

According to economists, since 1854, the U.S.A. has encountered 32 cycles of expansions and contractions, with an average of 17 months of contraction and 38 months of expansion.[1]

~ Wikipedia

Real estate values typically move slower than stocks,

commodities or other types of markets, and typically (but not always) real estate holds its value, with appreciation usually expected or planned for. But as you may know - maybe from your own experience– timing and the ability to ride a downturn are key.

There have been numerous studies showing that by having real estate in your portfolio, your returns can be stabilized and boosted than a portfolio without real estate (these typically refer to REITs but could just as well refer to direct ownership of real estate). Real estate is less volatile in general. But that doesn't mean that it is 'safe', 'guaranteed' or without any risk. Talk to an investor who purchased at the height of the market, lost tenants and may have stress meeting debt service, and you can understand one risk. But talk to an investor who bought during the dips, or in a stressed period, and this opportunity buyer will have a glowing story to tell.

The truth is that buyers will buy and sellers will sell at all different points of time. Investors made purchases when interest rates were soaring at 18% in the 80's and made the deals work as much as the investors who purchased at a 5.5% interest rate. Smart choices and good due diligence play a role in making a good acquisition.

Real estate is often favored by investors because it can supply cash flow and tax benefits. Cash flow from tenant rents; tax benefits from depreciation and expenses. And of course, capital gains from the sale of investment real estate can be deferred through the 1031 tax deferred exchange.

RISK AND DEFAULT

A risk and default study was cited in <u>CIRE Magazine</u>, "Net-Leased Single-Tenant Risks" by George Renz.

An analysis of 100 NLST (Net Leased Single Tenant) deals was conducted. Out of 100 transactions with locations nationwide ranging in value from $322,000 to $9 million, only 6 (six) tenants filed bankruptcy or did not pay rent. The breakdown:

~ Of 70 investment-grade and national tenants, (0) no investment-grade tenants defaulted and only 1 (one) national tenant defaulted;

~ Of 30 franchisee, regional, and local tenants, 5 (five) defaulted.

Tenant financials and credit are essential, and what I often emphasize when discussing investments with clients. It is key to success, in my opinion, if continuing passive income is the #1 goal.

CHAPTER 5
A QUICKIE ON CAP RATES AND VALUATION

Capitalization rates, always referred to as Cap Rates in the NNN world, are quite simple. It's a type of valuation of your investment based on income. Cap rates represents the annual rate of return (all cash, not figuring in any leverage) of the sales or acquisition price.

Every NNN deal that is listed for sale has its Cap Rate noted so you can compare apples to apples (you can see what all Walgreens are listed for, what all Starbucks are selling for, what all Dollar Generals are listed for – and compare different types of NNN deals).

And with any 2 factors below, you can figure the third: annual passive income, sales price, cap rate.

The formula is simple:

ANNUAL INCOME / SALE PRICE = CAP RATE

ANNUAL INCOME / CAP RATE = SALES PRICE

SALES PRICE X CAP RATE = ANNUAL INCOME

Example

Sale Price= $3,500,00
Annual income=$238,000

$238,000 / $3,500,000 = 6.8% Cap Rate

VALUATION

Investors who are stepping into the NNN world for the first time, may be used to evaluation of real estate in the traditional way (price per square foot, comps with local properties & sales.)

In fact, appraisers have three typical methods of evaluation:

the cost approach, the sales comp approach, and the income capitalization approach.

NNN properties are always evaluated with the income capitalization approach, using the formula above. When you investing in a net leased property, your focus is on the income the property will bring.

Some properties are WAY off and very high on the price per square foot appraisal, and that sometimes strikes those with real estate experience in other niches. But the whole point and focus on the net-leased world is INCOME.

Now, this is not to say that you shouldn't look at all of the factors involved in your investment – property age and condition, what the tenant is planning to do and the tenant credit-worthiness to get it done (and pay the various property expenses), the geographics and neighborhood, including other retail properties, barriers to entry, the trends and needs of the location, what other retail centers may be built, traffic counts, etc. to give you the full picture. This is really more in the due diligence part of your study, but it plays to valuation as well.

In general, investors want to evaluation the purchase price cap rate, any possible negotiation on that price, the value and expected income from the property in light of the rating of the tenant, lease term and lease details that dominate your investment.

During due diligence, factor in all of the rest to help make the decision to purchase.

CHAPTER 6
WHY A BUYER'S BROKER HELPS YOUR SUCCESS
HOW THESE TRANSACTIONS WORK

Every NNN property for sale (or virtually all) will have a listing broker. That broker's responsibility is to his seller, to get the deal done, to get the best price and to aid in the closing. While a buyer can deal directly with a selling broker, the buyer's interests are not represented.

A buyer's broker is responsible to you, the buyer, representing you and your interests. A good buyer's broker will work with you from beginning to closing of a successful transaction. A good broker will find out your situation, what kinds of goals you have for your acquisition (passive income, hold period, etc.), what dislikes you may have as regards tenants, industries or locations, where geographically you want your investment to be, what kind of debt and equity you need to replace, what kind of leverage you expect, your time line, and more.

Typically, the buyer's broker is paid by the Seller and Listing Broker, in a share of the Listing Broker's commission. In other words, with most deals, you work with the buyer's broker but do not pay him or her.

The broker will find a number of properties to present to you, fulfilling objectives and discussing the basics. The buyer's broker will do the Letter of Intent with basic terms on the property or properties of interest, to present to the selling broker. A contract will be presented if a Letter of Intent is accepted. (Many NNN brokers have a ready-made standard contract ready to go, but in some states there may be variances.) Stipulation on dates and times for due diligence, the materials to be provided in due diligence, when the contract goes hard (non-refundable), closing dates, and all other typical contractual language is included.

The title company, Qualified intermediary, your attorney (if you have one) and accountant will be involved at different times. Bank applications and paperwork are involved. Study of the title, survey, lease, and all important documents are done during due diligence. You may want to visit the property.

In the NNN world, due diligence can be as short as 2 weeks.

If the transaction involves a NN or property whereby you will be responsible for some items, due diligence on those items (such as roof) are imperative. How old is the roof, what is the condition, is there a warranty from the roofer and is it still under that warranty?

For tenants that are publicly-listed and rated, the financials are easily available. For other tenants, are the financials available, showing the net worth and financial capability? What about the store sales (monthly/annually) – are they available, and will they be reported to you during your hold period? (Some will, some won't.)

The most important evaluation is of the lease. What is the guarantee? What happens in the event of a fire or flood? Do they hold insurance which names you, and how much liability insurance do they hold? What are the terms at the end of the lease – what is the deadline that they must inform you if they intend to renew the lease? Are there terms about the lease renewal stated? What is definition of breach and remedies?

NNN leases are "take it or leave it" – there are no negotiations on terms. So study it closely – I always recommend an attorney but the broker can help point out issues.

Property Taxes & Insurance

Most NNN leases stipulate that the tenant will pay these bills and furnish the landlord with proof of payment. However, some leases will stipulate that you, the landlord, will pay these items and then submit the materials for reimbursement from the tenant. Some tax authorities require that the landlord be listed so the bill comes to you, and you then forward it for action to your tenant.

Some lenders will require that you take insurance or additional insurance on top of what the lease and tenant hold. This is on a transaction-by-transaction basis. If the tenant is not an S&P rated corporate entity, they may even require insurance to cover the mortgage should the tenant fail.

The key point here is that a good buyer's broker and team (your attorney & Qualified Intermediary among them), will help you review and understand the lease terms and your intended acquisition.

AN IDEAL TIMELINE TRANSACTION

You decide to sell an investment property you own and put it up for sale. You include language in your contract about an intended 1031.

You contact a buyer's broker. You discuss the amount of debt and equity you are expecting from your sale, the kind of NNN you may prefer and other details. The broker will start to look for properties for you. You start to look at the details, and see good candidates for acquisition (even though they might not be available when you are ready to make offers.)

Offers are coming in on your property and you decide to accept one. The buyer takes some time but accepts, and you sign a contract. You now know the general date of your closing.

You move into high gear on replacement options. Your broker, after seeing if any other candidate properties are also available, makes Letter of Intent offers on three of your favorites. Two accept, and you decide to proceed with one. The buyer is aware of your 1031, that you should close on X date to have 1031 funds.

You move to sign the contract and start due diligence on your intended acquisition, all the time going through the same as seller on your own investment property.

You move past your "hard" date on the deal you are selling, and know that you will close with relative confidence. This allows you to "go hard" on your NNN contract (move from the refundable to the non-refundable stage with completion of due diligence and intent to close) and lock in the deal.

Your investment property sells and your 1031 funds (sales proceeds) are handled by the QI, held in escrow. You now have 45 days to identify what you intend to purchase for the 1031 exchange. You officially "identify" what you intend to purchase (the property you are in contract on, and 2 backups on the broker's list.)

Two weeks later, you close on your NNN deal.

This is an ideal transaction. <u>However, they are not always ideal!</u> First, the sale of your investment property could fail, could be delayed, or could fall out of contract. Next, you could have a hard time getting the NNN you want due to competition. Or you are the 1st backup while awaiting another buyer to decide if the will proceed. Or you could go into contract on a NNN but then find in due diligence that there is a deal-breaker situation. There are so many variations of the time line above that could occur, but planning and foresight can help tremendously.

TIP – never go hard (past the refundable stage) on a NNN acquisition until you have done so on your investment sale. You may be able to extend a closing date for your NNN if your own sale has been delayed, but you can't break the contract without losing your deposit (which is typically sizable). This is where much of the stress comes in on these transactions!

Now, you might decide to not even start the "looking" process until the day (OK, maybe the week before) you close on your investment property (some take this route). But then the stress is on FINDING CANDIDATE PROPERTIES, GETTING THEM TIED UP IN A LETTER OF INTENT, GETTING INTO CONTRACT AND DOING DUE DILIGENCE BEFORE your 45 day ID period comes. Remember that ID countdown starts the day you sell your investment property. If a loan is in the mix, then the timing is even more difficult (the time to get approved is not swift).

TIP – if you are applying for a loan for your NNN deal, try to get a loan phrase in the contract regarding extension of the non-refundable period until the loan is approved…even if you sign off on the rest of due diligence. If you are able to be pre-approved with a bank, or have a relationship with a bank so that things can be expedited, all the better.

Know that all-cash deals almost always win out when competing for a property. Sellers will take an easy close – no delay, all-cash transaction over the unknown delays or potential non-approval of a lender deal.

Because NNN deals are competitive, not as plentiful as they once were and in demand, you might not be able to get what you want, or get it tied up in time. Planning is key, and working with your broker is a big help. They will be your ally in the trenches.

Triple Net investments are worthy passive-income investments, and deferring taxes when acquiring them can make a difference to your bottom line.

I trust that this overview will help arm you for conducting such a transaction!

If you have any questions about NNN investments, or would like a consultation, you can call the following number to set up a time: 1-866-891-1031 or email: info@kathyheshelow.com or visit: www.LegacyNNN.com

Thank you, Kathy Heshelow

P.S. I thank you in advance for leaving a short review about the book!

65000629R00036